BIG BUCK BU$INESS

ENERGY FOR EVERYONE?
THE BUSINESS OF ENERGY

by Nick Hunter

Gareth Stevens
Publishing

Please visit our website, www.garethstevens.com. For a free color catalog of all our high-quality books, call toll free 1-800-542-2595 or fax 1-877-542-2596.

Library of Congress Cataloging-in-Publication Data

Hunter, Nick.
Energy for everyone? : the business of energy / Nick Hunter.
    p. cm. — (Big-buck business)
Includes index.
ISBN 978-1-4339-7752-7 (pbk.)
ISBN 978-1-4339-7753-4 (6-pack)
ISBN 978-1-4339-7751-0 (library binding)
1. Energy industries—Juvenile literature. I. Title.
HD9502.A2H94 2013
333.79—dc23

                              2011052138

First Edition

Published in 2013 by
Gareth Stevens Publishing
111 East 14th Street, Suite 349
New York, NY 10003

© 2013 Gareth Stevens Publishing

Produced by Calcium Creative Ltd
Designed by Nick Leggett
Edited by Sarah Eason and Vicky Egan
Picture research by Susannah Jayes

Photo credits: Cover: Shutterstock: Kayros Studio l, N.Minton cr, Mirounga cl, Valdis Torms tcr.
Inside: Dreamstime: Robert Young 15t; Library of Congress: 8br, 9br, 10cr; Shutterstock: Asharkyu 13tr,
Sergei Bachlakov 31b, Darren Brode 43t, Chonlapoom 26b, Songquan Deng 12b, Tad Denson 3br, 20tr,
Patrik Dietrich 19tr, Elnur 14–15b, esbobeldijk 42bl, Left Eyed Photography 24r, Chris H. Galbraith 30tr,
Richard Griffin 11tr, haak78 10–11b, Steve Heap 44cr, Monkey Business Images 32b, 35br, Jaddingt 33cl,
Jordache 27l, Oleksandr Kalinichenko 18–19b, Kayros Studio 1tl, Christopher Kolaczan 37t, John Kroetch
39l, Oleksiy Mark 40bl, Ilja Mašík 5tr, Sue McDonald 41r, Caitlin Mirra 44l, Christopher Parypa 4b,
WDG Photo 28l, Rtem 17t, Veronika Rumko 5tr, Brad Sauter 16r, Jeff Schultes 6bl, Dalibor Sevaljevic 22b,
Silverkblack 23t, Vasily Smirnov 34–35tc, Michel Stevelmans 7l, Tish1 25c, Liviu Toader 13bl,
Jeff Wilber 38cr, Ahmad Faizal Yahya 36b, Eldad Yitzhak 29b; US Coastguard: Petty Officer First Class
John Masson 21bl.

Printed in the United States of America

CPSIA compliance information: Batch #CS12GS: For further information contact Gareth Stevens, New York, New York at 1-800-542-2595.

CONTENTS

POWER FOR THE PEOPLE

Energy is essential for all life. We eat food to give us the energy we need to run, jump, work, and play. The products and machines that we use every day also need energy to make them work. Automobiles and other vehicles get their energy from burning gasoline in their engines. Lights and other electrical appliances run on electricity, which is generated in power plants and brought to your home by power cables.

Big business

Energy is one of the world's biggest and most important industries. The energy business encompasses everything from finding energy sources, such as coal and oil, to supplying the energy needed to run your television or computer. This book looks at what the industry does, how it makes money, and what challenges it faces in the future.

Huge amounts of coal must be burned to create the electricity used in our cities.

IN THE NEWS

The energy industry is often in the news. Environmental campaigners accuse the industry of damaging the environment. People also complain when electricity and gasoline prices rise too high. However, they can do little to change the energy industry because their cars and homes depend on the energy it provides.

CHAPTER 1

THE RISE OF THE ENERGY INDUSTRY

People have always needed energy to keep them warm. Hundreds of years ago, this energy usually came from burning wood on an open fire. Ships at sea were powered by wind energy, and vehicles got the energy they needed to move from the horses that pulled them. We still use horsepower as a measure of how much energy an engine can produce.

Before the invention of the engine, vehicles were powered by animals such as horses or cattle.

Today, huge amounts of energy in the form of gasoline are consumed by our engine-powered cars.

The Industrial Revolution

Energy began to be big business during a period known as the Industrial Revolution. This began about 1750 in Great Britain and soon spread to other countries in Europe and North America.

Production speeds up

During the Industrial Revolution, new machines were invented that made it possible for factories to produce large quantities of goods, such as clothing and all sorts of metal products, very quickly. These new machines ran on steam power. Coal was used to heat up water to make the steam.

FUTURE FACT

The amount of energy that the world uses today has increased dramatically since the early days of steam power. There are nearly 1 billion vehicles on the roads, and this number continues to rise as India and China become richer.

BIRTH OF THE ENERGY INDUSTRY

In the early 1800s, steam power began to be used in transportation. Before long, railroads were built linking cities, and later they crossed whole continents. Steamships began to transport passengers across the oceans. By 1900, more than nine-tenths of the energy used by industry came from coal, and coal mining companies became some of the world's biggest businesses.

To satisfy the demand for coal, even children were recruited to work in the mines.

SMOG

The growing energy industry rapidly changed the world. Fumes from coal burned by industry caused smog, a thick haze of fog combined with smoke, which blackened buildings and choked the air. Many people suffered health problems as a result. We are now also discovering that burning fossil fuels, such as coal, has a long-term impact on climate (see pages 19 and 37).

Electricity and gas

Gas made from coal provided street lighting in the growing cities of the Industrial Revolution. Coal was also essential for producing electricity. The first coal-fired power stations were opened by Thomas Edison in London, Great Britain, and New York City in 1882.

This image from 1896 shows Oil City, founded at the mouth of Oil Creek.

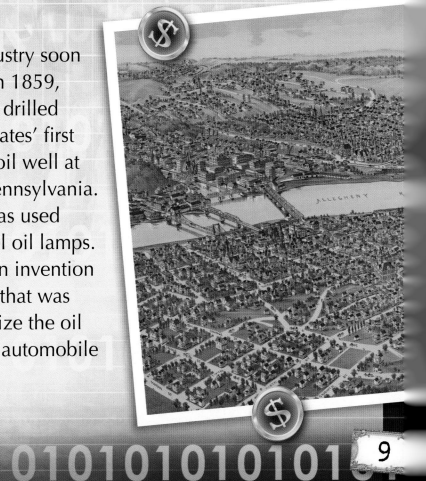

Striking oil

The coal industry soon had a rival. In 1859, Edwin Drake drilled the United States' first commercial oil well at Oil Creek, Pennsylvania. At first, oil was used mainly to fuel oil lamps. Then came an invention in the 1890s that was to revolutionize the oil industry. The automobile was born.

TRANSPORTATION AND TYCOONS

With the birth of the automobile in the 1890s came the need for a new energy source. Coal was fine for the large steam engines used to power trains and ships but was not suitable for automobiles, with their smaller engines. Gasoline, which is made from oil, proved the ideal fuel for the automobile's internal combustion engine.

Henry Ford became one of the first tycoons of the 20th century.

Money in oil

Early automobiles were expensive and unreliable. In 1900, there were only 8,000 in the whole United States. Sales took off when, in 1908, Henry Ford launched the Model T. This was a mass-produced car that ordinary people could afford to buy. As sales of automobiles soared and engines using oil-based fuels became standard in ships and aircraft, the corporations and business leaders that controlled the supply of oil grew very rich. Probably the most famous of these oil tycoons was John D. Rockefeller of the Standard Oil Company.

FUTURE FACT

Nuclear power generates about 13 percent of the world's electricity. If this amount is to increase in the future, the energy industry will have to find solutions to nuclear power's high costs and safety issues.

Nuclear power plants could potentially supply huge amounts of energy.

THE MODERN WORLD

Coal and oil are the most important sources of energy today. Companies and countries that control supplies of oil and coal can make big profits by selling their resources to people who need energy.

The rise of gas

Natural gas and oil are both fossil fuels and are often found together. In the past, the natural gas was burned off, and only the oil was extracted, because the gas was considered less useful than the oil and too difficult to transport. Today, however, natural gas is transported via pipelines and makes up about a quarter of the world's energy supply.

In hot areas that receive a lot of sunshine, solar power is a useful alternative energy source.

Desert cities such as Las Vegas use large amounts of energy just to keep buildings and cars cool enough for people to live there.

GAS WARS

Gas pipelines from Russia cross Ukraine to supply gas to western Europe. In 2009, an argument between Russia and Ukraine led to Russia switching off the supply of natural gas for two weeks. This cut the supply to Europe during freezing weather and showed how important it is for the energy industry to remain stable.

Alternative energy sources

In 2011, the world's population reached 7 billion people, and it continues to rise. As it rises, the demand for energy also increases. The energy industry needs to exploit all available forms of energy, not just fossil fuels, to meet the growing demand. This has led to an increased focus on alternative sources of energy, such as solar and wind power.

CHAPTER 2

ENERGY EXPLORATION

Raw materials are the backbone of the energy industry. To meet the world's growing energy needs, the energy industry has to find the raw materials needed to generate energy. Those raw materials may be used to power automobiles, ships, and aircraft, or to generate electricity for your home.

High risks, high costs

Searching for fossil fuels and extracting them from deep beneath Earth's surface involves huge costs. Many fossil fuels are found in places with extreme climates and deep under the ocean bed. The people who extract the fuel must work in very difficult and dangerous conditions, such as on oil platforms far out at sea.

All the oil in some areas has been extracted. These oil wells around Baku, Azerbaijan, are now deserted.

The search for oil is now taking place in some of the most extreme parts of the planet, such as the Arctic.

New technology

As well as paying for fossil fuel exploration and extraction, the energy industry must also pay for the technology needed to use other forms of energy, such as nuclear and solar energy.

FUTURE FACT

Fossil fuels are nonrenewable energy sources—once they have been extracted, they are gone for good. People are worried that the oil industry has only discovered enough oil to last for the next few decades.

KING

COAL

For many industries, coal is the most important source of energy. Much of the electricity that we use in our homes is generated by coal-fired power stations. Coal is also used to produce coke, a refined form of coal. Coke is burned to provide the heat needed to extract molten iron from iron ore. Coal is also used to make cement, which is important in the building of roads, bridges, and buildings.

Thousands of tons of coal are transported by trains across the United States.

Today, underground coal mining relies on machinery rather than manpower.

DANGER!

In the past men, women, and even children mined for coal in very unpleasant and dangerous conditions. Today, most mining is done by huge cutting machines, which is safer and more efficient. Disasters do still happen, though. In 2010, 29 miners in West Virginia were killed by an explosion 1,000 feet underground.

Surface mines

Every year, the energy industry mines about 7 billion tons of coal. Most of it comes from China, the United States, India, and Australia. Although we think of coal as coming from deep underground, it is also extracted from huge surface mines, where it lies close to ground level. About two-thirds of the coal mined in the United States comes from surface mines. Surface mining is less expensive than other mining, and more coal can be mined by each worker.

THE SEARCH FOR OIL AND GAS

Oil is not just an essential fuel for transportation. It is also important in the petrochemical industry, which produces plastics, cleaning products, and many other materials from oil. Oil companies employ geologists to look for underground rock formations that may contain oil. An oil well is then drilled to reach the oil and bring it to the surface.

Oil tankers are used to transport millions of gallons of oil across the oceans.

NO SMOKING

BE ALERT-AVOID POLLUTION   WORK SAFELY-PREVENT ACCIDENT

SAFETY FIRST

DANGEROUS CARGO

The oil business

Much of the world's oil and gas is found beneath the deserts of countries in the Middle East. Saudi Arabia, Iran, and the United Arab Emirates have all grown wealthy by exporting their oil. Elsewhere in the world, giant multinational corporations, such as Exxon, Shell, and BP, search and drill for oil in many different locations.

Countries such as the United Arab Emirates have huge reserves of oil.

FUTURE FACT

By burning fossil fuels, we are changing the climate. The gases that coal and oil give off when burned change the makeup of Earth's atmosphere. To try to stop climate change, governments are backing the search for alternative fuels.

DEEP-SEA OIL EXPLORATION

The first oil discovery from an off-shore well drilled out of sight of land was made in 1947. Since then, new technology has enabled the oil industry to look for oil under the seabed in deeper and deeper water. Oil wells can now be drilled under thousands of feet of water. Satellite technology allows oil companies to track and maintain the position of drilling rigs and oil platforms, as the water is too deep for them to rest on the seabed. The oil wells and pipes are repaired by robot submarines.

It costs billions of dollars to place and maintain deep-sea oil platforms like this one in the Gulf of Mexico.

Covering the cost

All this technology makes drilling for oil in deep water very expensive, so why do oil companies do it? You might think that the more they spend, the less money they will make from selling the oil. However, world demand for oil is so great that the oil companies need to keep looking for new oil reserves. To cover their costs, they charge their customers more. A high oil price makes deep-sea drilling worthwhile.

If just a small fault during oil drilling occurs, it can cause an explosion and an enormous fire, like that of the Deepwater Horizon.

DISASTER!

In 2010, an explosion and fire on the Deepwater Horizon drilling rig in the Gulf of Mexico killed 11 workers. Millions of gallons of oil leaked from the damaged well, killing seabirds and marine life and affecting fishing and tourism. The oil company BP and other companies involved had to pay out billions of dollars in compensation.

NUCLEAR POWER

Nuclear power is a very costly source of energy. The nuclear industry relies on relatively small amounts of rare metals, such as uranium and plutonium. The costs come in the technology needed to make energy from these raw materials and to keep people and the environment safe from the tiny particles of harmful radiation that are released by the fuel.

Radiation risk

Nuclear power is attractive to many governments because it does not contribute to climate change. However, many people are concerned about the risks to health and the environment from radiation leaks and the disposal of fuel, which can remain dangerous for hundreds of years. These risks, and the costs involved in protecting against them, mean that many energy companies prefer to invest in coal- and gas-fired power plants, which are cheaper.

Nuclear power is likely to supply more and more of our energy in decades to come.

The toxic symbols on this nuclear fuel container warn of the radiation dangers inside.

NUCLEAR DISASTER

In 2011, a tsunami hit Japan and damaged the Fukushima nuclear power plant, which released dangerous radiation. Some 80,000 people had to leave their homes. Billions of dollars were paid in compensation, but it may be many years before the true cost of the disaster is known.

23

ALTERNATIVE ENERGY

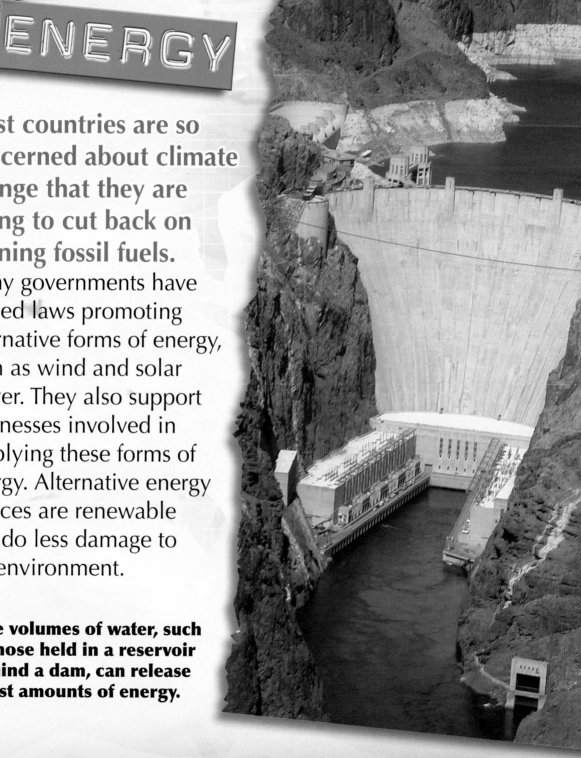

Most countries are so concerned about climate change that they are trying to cut back on burning fossil fuels. Many governments have passed laws promoting alternative forms of energy, such as wind and solar power. They also support businesses involved in supplying these forms of energy. Alternative energy sources are renewable and do less damage to the environment.

Huge volumes of water, such as those held in a reservoir behind a dam, can release vast amounts of energy.

Water power

Hydroelectricity is the most commonly used form of alternative energy. It is usually generated by river water being released from a reservoir behind a dam. As the water falls with tremendous force, it spins the blades of giant turbines that power the generators that make electricity.

Biofuels, like other forms of renewable energy, remain a small part of the energy industry.

Fuel from plants

Biofuels are fuels made from crops. They can be mixed with fossil fuels and used in vehicle engines. The main drawback with biofuels is that they take up land that could be used for growing food.

CHAPTER 3

ENERGY SUPPLY

An energy source first has to be transported to the country where it is needed. Then it must be changed into a form of energy that can easily be used by people, whether in factories, homes, or for transportation.

Transportation

Most of the fuels used to generate electricity in the United States and Europe are carried there by long pipelines or by ship. Transporting oil, coal, and gas in huge ships is an industry in itself.

Electricity is carried from power stations to buildings along cables.

Where does the energy go?

The energy industry produces energy for three main groups:

• **Industry:** Factories and businesses need electricity to run everything from computers and lighting to specialized machinery. Coal is used to heat furnaces and oil is used to run vehicles.

• **Residential use:** Electricity is needed to run everything from kitchen appliances to lighting. Many homes also use gas for cooking and gas or oil for heating.

• **Transportation:** Automobiles, large ships, and even spacecraft depend on oil. Some trains use oil, while others are powered by electricity.

Many manufacturing businesses use huge furnaces to create goods. They are powered by large amounts of coal.

POWER GENERATION

We take it for granted that when we flick a switch, electricity will be provided. Making sure energy is available when we want to use it is a complex process.

Making electricity

Electricity is generated when an energy source is used to turn a turbine, which powers a generator. Hydroelectricity uses water to turn the turbine, and wind power uses the wind. In most power plants, steam power is used. The steam comes from water that has been heated by nuclear power or by burning coal or gas. The water turns to steam, and the steam turns the turbine, which generates electricity.

BLACKOUT

In 2003, many parts of the northeastern United States, including New York City, and Canada had blackouts. Poor maintenance of the cables and other parts of the electricity grid were blamed on the companies responsible for the grid.

The grid

Electricity is carried from power plants to homes and businesses by a system of cables and other equipment called the grid. Utility companies manage the grid. They need to ensure that enough power is in the grid at peak times, such as when people are cooking their evening meal. The utility companies can buy energy from each other to supply their customers.

Wind turbines must be positioned in areas where there is plenty of wind, such as on hilltops.

Geothermal power stations such as this one use the energy created by underground hot springs to generate electricity.

ENERGY FOR TRANSPORTATION

The fuel that powers most transportation is oil. However, you can't just put crude oil (the raw material that comes out of the ground) into an engine and expect it to run. First it has to be separated into different products, such as gasoline for automobiles and kerosene for aircraft. This refined fuel is carried in tanker trucks from the oil refinery to gas stations and major users, such as airports.

If the price of refined fuel such as kerosene becomes too expensive, it could put an airline out of business.

The auto racing car business relies on highly refined gasoline to power its cars.

Demand for oil is rising all the time as industry develops and more and more people own cars. If the world's oil supply declines in future years, as some people believe it will, but demand rises, prices will rise, too.

The price of oil

The price customers pay for gasoline changes frequently. Traders on markets such as the New York Mercantile Exchange (NYMEX) buy and sell contracts for oil. The price goes up and down for lots of reasons. In cold weather, more people want oil for heating, so the price goes up. Businesses that use a lot of fuel, such as airlines, try to agree upon prices a long way in advance so they know what their fuel will cost the following year.

ENERGY FOR HOMES AND BUSINESSES

Have you ever had a power blackout at home?
If you have, you'll know just how much we rely on energy.
As well as using electricity, which is provided at the flick
of a switch, many homes also use oil and natural gas for
heating and cooking. Most domestic energy is used to
keep homes warm in winter and cool in summer.

**Rising costs make buying
energy one of the most
expensive monthly bills.**

Paying for energy

Energy is a big cost for every household. Utility companies calculate how much energy we use by fitting a meter in our home. Every few months, they send out a bill for the amount of electricity and gas that we have used.

Solar panels can reduce the cost of other energy bills.

Double-paned windows and insulation prevent heat loss and can help reduce fuel bills.

ENERGY AND PRICES

One reason why the cost of everyday goods goes up is because the cost of making the product goes up. If fuel prices rise, the cost of electricity used in factories goes up, and the cost of transporting products to stores goes up, too. This means that you, the consumer, have to pay more.

Many houses are now built in ways that help save energy and keep costs down.

Hidden cost

We spend money on energy every time we buy something in a store or online. The price that a business charges for goods and services includes a percentage of the energy costs that they have to pay.

CHAPTER 4

THE BIG PLAYERS

The business of generating energy from raw materials and transporting it to consumers is a huge and complex industry. Delivering a reliable electricity supply and finding new supplies of fuel costs the energy industry billions of dollars.

Energy giants

The fact that every home, business, and vehicle needs energy means that the energy industry is one of the biggest on Earth. Exxon Mobil, the largest of the major oil companies, is the world's second-biggest company by revenue. Only the shopping giant Walmart makes more money. Other energy giants feature heavily in the list of the world's largest companies.

TOO MUCH POWER?

The energy giant ExxonMobil makes more money in a year than all the money that comes into a small country like Belgium in a year through sales and taxes. Some people think the size and wealth of the big energy companies give them too much influence over governments.

The increasing use of cars around the world has driven the growth of energy companies.

Billions of dollars are traded on the stock exchange as people buy and sell energy company stocks and shares.

OPEC

The Organization of Petroleum Exporting Countries (OPEC), which includes Saudi Arabia, Iran, Nigeria, and Venezuela, can control oil prices by increasing or reducing the amount of oil they produce. Most OPEC countries are in the Middle East and Africa, but their decisions affect energy users across the world.

BIG OIL

Many multinational oil companies make it onto the list of the world's biggest corporations. Among them are the US giants ExxonMobil, Chevron, and Conoco Philips. The "big oil club" also includes Shell, BP, Total, and PetroChina.

Nationals and multinationals

The major international oil companies have exploration, refining, and sales operations in many countries around the world. They are also leading the search for oil in new places, such as under the ocean bed in very deep water and under the Arctic. Despite their huge size, multinational oil companies control only about one-tenth of the world's known oil reserves. Most oil is controlled by national oil companies, such as Saudi Arabia's Saudi Aramco.

The next time you refuel your car at a gasoline station, look out for the "big oil club" names.

At this reserve in Alberta, Canada, oil is being extracted from surface sand to help fulfill the demand for fuel.

Justifying their size

Big oil companies are often criticized by environmental campaigners and others for their actions and for the huge profits they make. The oil companies argue that they are just meeting the demand for oil. They have to be big to afford the huge costs of finding new energy reserves.

CLIMATE DEBATE

At first, the big oil companies questioned the link between burning fossil fuels and climate change. As the evidence became more widely accepted, they publicly ended their funding of groups that denied the existence of climate change.

UTILITY

COMPANIES

Each country usually has its own utility companies, unlike energy companies, which may operate in several different countries. The biggest utility companies serve regions with very large populations. Others serve small areas with few people.

Power for the people

The world's largest utility company is Germany's E.ON, which provides electricity to customers across Europe. In the United States, there are more than 3,000 utility companies. The largest include Exelon Corporation of Chicago, Illinois, and the Southern Company in the southeastern states.

People can monitor the amount of energy they are using in their homes with an energy meter.

Utility companies must maintain the poles and cables that carry electricity to homes and businesses.

Price watch

Many customers have a limited choice as to which utility companies they can use. Regulators keep a close watch on prices to make sure that utilities do not overcharge their customers.

FUTURE FACT

In 2011, Boeing unveiled its new 787 Dreamliner aircraft, which is said to use 20 percent less fuel than other aircraft. Developments such as this will help to determine how much energy we use in the future.

CHAPTER 5

CHANGING ENERGY INDUSTRY

The energy industry is constantly changing.
It has come a long way since the days of the Industrial Revolution, when energy was first needed to power factories and mechanized transportation. In the 20th century, a growing demand for oil and the discovery of nuclear energy changed the energy industry forever.

Changing trends

Businesses must adapt to meet their customers' needs, otherwise the customers will buy the product they want from someone else. As costs of energy have risen, many customers have started buying vehicles and other products that use less energy.

Transportation industries are constantly exploring technology and new forms of energy that could reduce fuel costs.

Under pressure to change

Energy companies may face demands for change if they cause damage to the environment, as happened in 2010 when a massive oil spill polluted the Gulf of Mexico. The energy industry is also under pressure to use more renewable energy sources to help combat the threat of climate change.

Making some trips by bike instead of by car can help cut your energy use.

FUTURE FACT

What can people do to reduce their energy bills in the future? Use less energy! Fitting more insulation in the home to prevent heat escaping and turning off air conditioning when people go out will both help cut costs.

RENEWABLE ENERGY BUSINESSES

There is big money to be made in renewable energy. Billionaire businessman Zhengrong Shi is the proof. His company Suntech is the world's biggest maker of solar panels, which convert energy from the sun into electricity.

Renewable energy could be big-buck business for many future tycoons.

Wind of change

Supported by a network of investors, renewable or "Green Tech" businesses have seen big growth since 2000. One wind turbine manufacturer believes that one-tenth of the world's energy industry will be in renewable energy by 2020.

solar panels

Clean cars

The automotive industry is spending money on new technologies. Hybrid cars combine a regular engine with an electric motor. They have become popular with consumers who want to save fuel. Automobiles powered by hydrogen fuel cells are also being developed. These cars do not release the gases that cause climate change. Many experts believe they may eventually replace gasoline-powered cars, but first a network of hydrogen fuel stations will need to be built so the cars can fill up!

The manufacture of hybrid cars, and the supply of hydrogen energy, could be big business in decades to come.

CHALLENGES AHEAD

Perhaps the most important challenge for the energy industry is the threat of climate change. In many parts of the world, temperatures could rise so much that people will not be able to grow the food they need to live. Melting ice around the North and South Poles could cause sea levels to rise. Will the energy industry and governments around the world be able to act in time to stop this from happening?

Low-lying cities, such as New Orleans, will suffer from repeated flood damage if climate change continues.

India and China

India and China both have rapidly growing economies. As more and more people find they can afford cars and other products, the demand for energy soars. Will the energy industry be able to supply all the energy that is needed? Can it rely on oil and coal, which are not renewable?

Governments and the energy industry are exploring all forms of renewable energy, including tidal power.

Essential energy

Whatever the answers to these questions, a successful energy industry will remain essential. Without a good supply of energy, other industries cannot survive. Energy is at the heart of modern life, and the industry will continue to change to meet new challenges.

CLIMATE TARGETS

In 1997, most of the world's governments agreed upon targets to reduce emissions of the gases that cause climate change. The measure has been less successful than was hoped because some governments, including that of the United States, have not fully agreed to its rules.

GLOSSARY

alternative sources of energy energy other than fossil fuels

billion one thousand million, or 1,000,000,000

blackout when electricity supplies to buildings are cut off

climate long-term shift in weather and weather patterns, partly caused by human actions, such as burning fossil fuels

coal a fossil fuel created when plants that grew as long as 400 million years ago rotted down over millions of years

commercial a business that aims to make a profit

compensation money paid to someone in order to make up for a loss or damage

consumer anyone who buys or uses a product or service

corporation a huge organization often made up of many businesses

fossil fuel energy sources (coal, oil, and natural gas) formed from the decayed remains of living things

generate convert one form of energy into another

hydroelectricity electricity generated by using water power

hydrogen fuel cell a device that captures energy from the gas hydrogen

insulation material designed to prevent the transfer of heat

internal combustion engine a type of engine that creates power by burning fossil fuels such as oil

investor a person who puts money into a business in the hope of making a profit

natural gas a gas that occurs naturally on Earth and is not manufactured

nuclear power energy created through nuclear reaction

oil reserve oil found underground, but not yet brought to the surface

ore rock containing metal deposits

power station or power plant a place where energy is created

profit money that a business makes on top of the money it has spent in buying or producing something

radiation harmful particles that are released by the materials used in nuclear power

raw materials wood, water, coal, or any material as it is when it is found, before it has been changed by a process

refinery a place where a substance, such as crude oil, is separated into different parts

regulator a person or body that makes rules for how a business should be run

reserve a collection or supply of something that can be used later

reservoir a large reserve of water

revenue the money that a business receives when it sells something

solar power energy created by using heat from the sun's rays

tsunami an enormous wave

turbine a motor driven by steam or water power that generates electricity

FOR MORE INFORMATION

BOOKS

Coad, John. *Finding and Using Oil* (Why Science Matters series). Chicago, IL: Heinemann Library, 2008.

Flath, Camden. *Careers in Green Energy: Fueling the World with Renewable Resources*. Broomall, PA: Mason Crest, 2011.

Whiting, Jim. *The Science of Lighting a City: Electricity in Action* (Action Science series). Mankato, MN: Capstone, 2010.

WEBSITES

Find out more about energy and how we use it at:

www.eia.gov/kids

www.energyquest.ca.gov/story

www.dteenergy.com/kids/renewableEnergyville.html

www.seco.cpa.state.tx.us/seco_links-kids

INDEX